FROM THE MOUNTAINS TO THE SEA

Nic Bishop

From the Mountains to the Sea

The Secret Life of New Zealand's Rivers and Wetlands

REED

TO RON, GAY AND THE 'FAMILY'

Half-title:
Little shag (*Phalacrocorax melanoleucos*) dries its wings at the estuary margin.

Facing title:
A green tree frog (*Litoria raniformis*) can jump more than ten times its body length.

Published by Reed Books, a division of Reed Publishing (NZ) Ltd, 39 Rawene Road, Birkenhead, Auckland. Associated companies, branches and representatives throughout the world.

ISBN 0 7900 0347 3

Cover and text design by Chris Lipscombe.
Text set in Goudy Old Style.
Colour separations and printing by Everbest, Hong Kong.

CONTENTS

ACKNOWLEDGEMENTS

For help, encouragement or company while working on this book I would like to thank Roger Bartlett, Ben Bell (Victoria University of Wellington), Tim Dodgshun (University of Otago), Brian Frost, Nick Groves and Mary Rose (DOC), Tony Harris (Otago Museum), Lindsay Hasley (Southland Museum), Ian Jamieson (University of Otago), Gerry Kessells (DOC), Chris Lalas, Dave Murray (DOC), Iain Murray (ECNZ), Heather Newell (ECNZ), Derek Onley, Moira Parker, Horrie Sinclair, Mark Pickering, Mike Watkins (DOC), Ron Peacock (DOC) and Ian Woodhead.

My thanks also to friend and fellow nature photographer, George Chance, for allowing me to use the photographs featured on pages 66 and 90; and to Maria Jungowska, who edited the manuscript.

I have been grateful for the invaluable assistance of ECNZ while preparing this book. Budget Rent a Car Ltd and Intercity Coachlines kindly assisted in getting me to some of the locations.

Finally, I wish to thank my wife and companion, Vivien, for her assistance and encouragement throughout this project.

Nic Bishop
March 1994

AMONG THE ORCHIDS that grow in wetlands are species of sun orchid (*Thelymitra*). They grow from an undergound rhizome, sending up decorative sprays of flowers in late spring.

FOREWORD

THE WORK OF NATURE PHOTOGRAPHER Nic Bishop provides a fascinating record of life in and near New Zealand's waterways. His work shows a very high level of technical expertise and a warmth and respect for his subjects.

Nic's photographic skill offers a glimpse of the complex and often secretive world of the waterways. He achieved many of his stunning high-speed portraits by capturing his subjects on film at eye-level or lower. Often this meant he had to spend hours sitting or lying in deep swamp water in considerable discomfort.

The book follows the journey of water from the mountains to the sea, including the rivers, the wetlands and the estuaries. Throughout this journey Nic portrays the dynamics of ecosystems, the instrinsic value of wildlife and the aesthetic importance of nature.

The Electricity Corporation of New Zealand is proud to have supported Nic with this work. As an extensive user of natural resources, ECNZ strives to use those resources responsibly at all times. This is a key element of our environmental principles.

We believe this book will provide readers with a great deal of enjoyment, as well as helping to increase appreciation of this country's unique environment.

David Frow
Chief Executive
Electricity Corporation of New Zealand Limited

INTRODUCTION

ONE OF THE MOST POIGNANT MOMENTS of this century happened when, during the Apollo missions to the moon, astronauts turned their cameras back to photograph the Earth. At this moment when technology had triumphed in its bid to venture into space, we were given a compelling image of our one and only home, planet Earth, floating vivid yet vulnerable in the darkness. For humankind it was a coming of age, a timely reminder of the responsibility that lay with new-found power.

The azure-blue globe with swirls of white clouds also belied our anthropocentric vision of the world. Our 'Earth' is in fact a water planet. Water covers some seven-tenths of the Earth's surface, and it is the presence of liquid water that distinguishes our planet from all others in the Solar System. Life evolved in this aquatic environment some 3800 million years ago. The endless cycling of water through the atmosphere and within ocean currents distributes the massive heat influx that the world receives from the sun each day, moderating the climate and making it habitable.

This book is concerned with that fraction of the Earth's water which flows in rivers and wetlands. It is but the merest fraction, less than 0.03 percent of the total water present in the seas and frozen ice caps, yet this maintains all terrestrial life. Sometimes called 'Earth's blood', fresh water runs capillaries across the land, greening its surface and supporting diverse animal communities.

The following pages celebrate this phenomenon, revealing the life of New Zealand's rivers and wetlands. Rather than simply catalogue the species found here, I have concentrated on the aesthetic, wishing to produce images that draw the viewer to these waterscapes and into contact with the purposeful, self-willed lives of their inhabitants.

Neither have I gone in search of the rare or different. Many of the plants and animals featured here could be considered 'everyday'. They live in local rivers, swampy paddocks and small ponds, but are often overlooked in our hurried lives. In fact these creatures can be vulnerable because of being ordinary. While working on this book I have watched the progress of a housing subdivision expand towards my favourite dragonfly pond. When the drains are finally laid, few of the motorists that roar by each day will notice. But the pond will be lost to the insect life that thrives there, and to the pair of paradise shelducks that return each spring to raise their family. It will also be lost to the generations of children that paddle its soggy margins, catching frogs or studying tadpoles.

A river, a wetland or an estuary can be viewed as a discrete water world, each with its own living microcosm. The life of a backswimmer in an alpine tarn barely touches that of a mudfish in a swamp. Yet both are affected if it does not rain. Each of these habitats is linked in one continuum by the flow of water. Viewed this way, the journey of water to the sea serves as a metaphor for the natural world as a whole. The text of this book thus often travels beyond its immediate focus to address wider issues of conservation. Wonder lies not only in the lives of individuals, but also in their lives together as communities, and in communities threaded together in the life of one vital and prosperous water planet, gently turning through space.

SMALL TARNS ARE FOUND perched among even the steepest of mountain ranges, such as here in the Humboldt Mountains. Summer sun warms their shallow waters, transforming them into a microcosm of life. Insect larvae stir from the bottom and emerge as winged adults. Small spiders hunt the soggy margins and rafts of algae tint the surface.

THE MOUNTAINS

F OR MORE THAN A THOUSAND KILOMETRES, the west wind blows towards New Zealand unhindered by land. It sweeps the Tasman Sea, driven by prevailing weather systems that dominate southern latitudes, and as it moves it gathers water vapour, each molecule loosened from the rolling waves by the energy absorbed from sunlight. Then, like an aerial ocean, the air washes against the land. It sways the crowns of canopy trees and funnels through river gorges. Climbing and cooling, water vapour condenses to foaming cloud, then falling rain, drenching the mossy boughs of silver beech forest and finding voice in the roar of tumbling rivers.

Wind forces the air mass onwards, past snowfield and rock tor, until it spills over the crest of the dividing ranges. Falling, expanding, warming and picking up speed, it races eastwards over foothills and plains. By now the air can be more than four degrees warmer than when it first reached the western coastline, for each molecule of water vapour that condensed over the mountains has liberated latent heat — the heat from the sun that first caused it to evaporate from the sea. In Canterbury, where the warming and drying effect is greatest, the wind is known as the nor'wester. It is volatile and hungry. It steals moisture from plants, whips dust from the land and frays the nerves of otherwise sane people.

The powerful conjunction of mountains and moist westerlies defines the nature of New Zealand. It dictates the contrasts between east and west, determining differences in climate, the greenness of the land, the pattern of human settlement and the character of the inhabitants. The phenomenon also invests New Zealand with a wealth more lasting than gold. Agriculture, power generation, tourism — the economy of a nation — all depend in one way or another on the guarantee of a bountiful rainfall.

There is a price to pay for the bounty. Over ten metres of rain falls each year in New Zealand's wettest mountain regions, and downpours can drop more than thirty centimetres into catchments overnight, turning rivers to steel-grey monsters that uproot forests and spit the wreckage into the sea. This tyrannical will seems paradoxical, given the benign feel of falling rain and snow. Yet the profile of the land has been cut by water. Left to itself, water's abrasive touch would one day render the landscape to flat plains, washed over by the waves. But erosion is balanced by a slow lifting of the land. Tectonic forces of the past few million years have raised some twenty vertical kilometres of rock from the sea. Today, fewer than four of these remain standing in the summit of Mount Cook. The difference is the measure of the power of water.

Water held the peak of its tyranny during the Ice Age, starting some two million years ago. It is hard to imagine the crushing burden of ice that once lay upon the mountains. Under the pressure of its own weight this ice became 'plastic' and flowed downhill as glaciers. Moving several metres each day, the glaciers plucked rocks in their paths that acted as cutting tools to rasp out valley walls and truncate spurs. The results are best seen in Fiordland, where the resolute nature of the native rock, largely granite, has preserved the impression of ice. Here, valley walls are sheer, and sometimes even overhanging. To gaze at such masterworks and let the mind extrapolate back 15,000 years to the last glacial advance, is to perceive the breadth of nature's power.

Thankfully, this image rests only in our imaginings. Today, mountain lands are a picture of tussock expanses, lichened rocks and summer wildflowers. There are tawny greens, earth ochres and everywhere an orchestration of rushing streams. Given that mountains are synonymous with rainfall, it comes as a surprise to find that many alpine plants are adapted to drought. The reason is that thin, cool mountain air can hold relatively little water vapour and is very drying when it blows over sun-warmed surfaces. Added to this, steep rocky mountain soils drain quickly, providing meagre reservoirs of moisture from which vegetation can replenish its loss. In answer, most alpine plants hold their leaves close to the ground and cover them with sleek coats of felted white hair, so sheltering their vulnerable green surfaces from the drying wind.

The alpine world is thus one of contrast, of tall mountains and miniature plants. On exposed slopes you can tread on top of a 'canopy' of dwarf coprosma shrubs, dracophyllums and other plants whose lowland relatives would reach over your head. Life here, seemingly hardy and resilient, is in fact very vulnerable. A clumsy footing and the torn community can take decades of attenuated alpine summers to recover. Growth is more verdant wherever water flows freely. Sheltered stream-banks and wet seepages are smothered with alpine herbs, including ourisias, violets, anisotomes and snow marguerites, to name a few. And as reminder of how the natural world can turn topsy-turvy, there are giants of the plant world here, too. The giant mountain buttercup can grow leaves as big as dinner plates and flowers like porcelain saucers.

Elsewhere, on flat-topped ranges or in hollows, water remains trapped and stagnant. Here, poor drainage leads to deficiencies of oxygen and key mineral nutrients. This, combined with cool conditions, inhibits both growth and decay. Thus bogs support specialist plants that grow on dark peat soils comprising the poorly decomposed remains of countless prior generations. On first impression, these places seem bleak and monotonous, but tread carefully on the quivering ground and you will find the plant community is suprisingly varied and exquisite in its detail. White-flowering donatia, bog celmisia, red-berried pentachondra and a mosaic of other cushion plants cover the ground like a patchwork quilt. Protruding through the seams, millions of sundews hold out finger-like leaves to snare passing insects with droplets of sticky glue. The sundew digests the insect and extracts minerals from the spent body, making good the shortfall it experiences in the bog.

Every bog plant is adapted in some way to waterlogged conditions, but the success story of this environment is sphagnum moss. This green 'sponge' grows in the wettest parts, often bordering open water. It copes with the nutrient-poor conditions by having an extraordinary ability to snap up scarce mineral ions from the surrounding water. This, in turn, makes the environment so acidic that it becomes inimical to other organisms, including bacteria and fungi. In fact, sphagnum was relied on earlier this century for its antiseptic properties. During the First World War, British Army medical teams used as many as a million moss dressings per month. Sphagnum also has the ability of holding up to twenty-five times its weight in water, with the aid of countless microscopic pores on its surfaces. The moss can therefore carry its favoured soggy environment with it as it grows upwards, building new layers on its undecayed remains. In time, the swelling blanket spills sideways, smothering and often overwhelming other vegetation to extend across large tracts of flat-topped ranges.

The environment peculiar to sphagnum is home to a varied community of animal specialists. The number of species and the subtlety of their lives remain obscure, for many are cryptic and their habitat is remote. Limited investigations by entomologists have so far revealed wetas, moths, dragonflies, beetles and spiders, many of which are unique to this environment and so new to science. One recent find, a moth whose larvae burrow into the semi-aquatic quagmire, has been classified as a new species and new genus. Like several other sphagnum inhabitants, this moth also belongs to a particularly primitive group. Sphagnum-dominated ecosystems have been around for well over 200 million years, and are therefore likely haunts in which to turn up a 'tuatara' of the invertebrate world. It seems almost embarrassingly easy to uncover new species in places such as these. Sphagnum is just one of many habitats waiting for exploration by field biologists. In this age when technology can reach to the stars, we are oddly blind to the many uncharted living worlds at our feet.

Notwithstanding their value as habitats, these mountain wetlands are hidden water reservoirs. Their capacity to store water and release it at a steady rate cushions nearby lowlands from potentially damaging floods and droughts. High-country managers are wise to safeguard such a role and to leave the soggy mantle of vegetation 'undeveloped'. In haste to turn profit from the land, it is easy to send the costs downstream.

Benefit may also come from the tall snowgrass vegetation that covers much of the alpine zone. Research indicates that these native tussocks are very efficient at relaying water from highlands to lowlands, so increasing the flow output of catchments. It seems that of the rainfall they intercept, snowgrasses lose relatively little by evaporation in comparison to managed pasture. Their long leaf blades can also gather significant amounts of dew from the air, supplementing the water obtained from rain alone.

Arrayed far from the precincts of the urban landscape, mountains would seem to have only a distant bearing on daily life. For some, they offer a retreat, a last untouched place where the visitor must fall into tune with the dictates of the landscape and the amplitude of the seasons. These regions are also large enough and wild enough for the interplay of biological and physical processes to continue to unfold new life, whether in bright fields of alpine flowers or hidden confines of sphagnum bogs. The mountains do affect our lives directly, however, reaching us every day, each hour, at the twist of a tap. Cloud-makers and rain-givers, theirs is the gift of water.

▲
SUNRISE FLICKERS BRIEFLY on the eastern flanks of the Main Divide near Mount Cook as a storm rolls over from the west. Rising more than 3000 metres into moist winds that sweep off the Tasman Sea, the Southern Alps experience rapid and ferocious changes of weather.

WHEN SEABORNE WINDS touch the winter summit of Mount Taranaki, water vapour freezes directly out of the air into the solid state, encrusting rock surfaces with knobbly ice formations known as sastrugi. These can become very pronounced, growing into the wind as more ice is deposited. ▶

THE SNOW-FED WATERS OF
the Dobson River rush
down-valley on their long
journey from the
mountains to the sea.
River flows are low during
the winter as most of the
precipitation remains on
the ranges in frozen form.
It is a quiet time in the
hills, for many animals
have headed towards the
lowlands, while others lie
hidden in a torpid state.

ALPINE FLOWERS ARE often most prominent by stream banks, where water and nutrients are provided in abundance. Here one can expect to see fine displays of alpine foxgloves, giant mountain buttercups and parahebes. Among the most striking and abundant of flowering plants, however, are the alpine daises, or celmisias. There are over fifty types of celmisia in the alpine zone, varying much in their leaf shape, but all bearing the recognisable daisy flowerhead.

CLEAR WINTER NIGHTS leave an array of frosty forms by the water's edge. One can look in wonder at these fragile creations, as exquisite as any work of art, yet by mid-morning they will all be gone, victims to the sun.

WINTER LAYS A CARPET OF snow to the shoreline of Lake Mavora in the mountains of Southland. Like all major South Island lakes Mavora owes its creation to ice age glaciers, which scraped depressions in the valley floor and left moraine walls, damming river outflows.

JUST A FEW DAYS OLD, these paradise shelduck chicks (*Tadorna variegata*) still bear the egg tooth on the tip of their bill, which is used to chip their way to freedom during hatching. The parent birds are very protective of their brood and it is not uncommon to see the female herding away other birds, even large geese, as the family heads off on feeding trips.

ALTHOUGH IT IS ALSO found near lowland lakes and wetlands, most trampers and hunters will associate the paradise shelduck with the tussock riverflats of the high country. It is the most vocal of native waterfowl, taking to the air with a clamour of honking and shrieking at your approach. Paradise shelducks pair for life and the female can be distinguished by her white head, compared with the male's dark head.

ACTING AS A MINIATURE
wide-angle lens, each
raindrop holds a perfect
image of a celmisia flower.

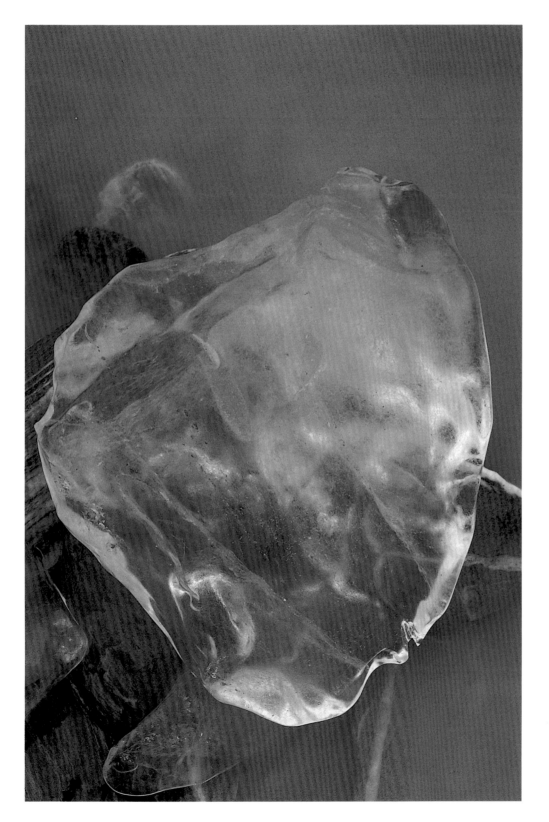

A LUMP OF GLACIAL ICE, the product of snowstorms perhaps more than a hundred years earlier, lies stranded by the Waiho River. When heavy rains fall on the western flanks of the Southern Alps, floodwaters build up pressure at bottlenecks within the Franz Josef Glacier. Sudden blowouts release blocks of ice downstream accompanied by frightening surges of river level.

Photographed at the moment of contact, a small fly snares its hind leg as it hurtles past a sundew (*Drosera arcturi*). Sundews are common in bogs and cope with the typical nutrient deficiency of their habitat by capturing insects. Leaves covered with sticky hairs hold fast to small animals that touch them. As the victim struggles to escape, other hairs curl round to secure it. The sundew digests its prey, absorbing precious mineral nutrients in the process.

ON FLATTER-TOPPED ranges, such as here on the Livingstone Range, there are extensive bogland communities. It is a world in miniature, with a surprisingly rich mosaic of specialist plants adapted to waterlogged and cold peaty conditions. A close look will reveal firm cushions of *Donatia novae-zelandiae*, turfs of cushion sedge (*Oreobolus pectinatus*) interspersed with the blooms of bog daisy (*Celmisia alpina*) and purple-flowered bladderworts (*Utricularia*). The wettest parts grow soggy blankets of sphagnum moss.

AMONG THE MORE conspicuous animals of the alpine tarn is the redcoat damselfly (*Xanthocnemis*). On warm days these damselflies are active by the water's edge, mating and laying eggs. The eggs are deposited in vegetation by the soggy margins of the tarn.

WITH A BODY LENGTH OF about 80 mm the giant mountain dragonfly (*Uropetala chiltoni*) is the biggest of New Zealand's dragonflies. When mating, dragonflies form a wheel as seen here. The male has grasped the female at the back of the head with a pair of special claspers on the tip of his abdomen. The female has arched her abdomen so that her genital pouch is in contact with the male's copulatory organ.

NEW ZEALAND BLUEBELLS (*Wahlenbergia albomarginata*) lift bell-shaped flowers above a carpet of small plants that have colonised a stony alpine riverbed. The flowerbuds develop in a sheltered microclimate near the ground and the elongating flower stem then pulls them up.

TIME IS ALL IT TAKES FOR
water to cut rock gorges,
such as this canyon in the
Kokatahi Valley in
Westland.

THE RIVERS

NEW ZEALAND IS A LAND OF RIVERS. High ranges and heavy rainfall collaborate to produce over 200,000 kilometres of major river channels, carrying water in perpetual pursuit of the sea. Most rush headlong in their journey, making few diversions *en route*. The longest river, the Waikato, measures some 400 kilometres, which is modest in world terms. But then the reputation of New Zealand rivers does not lie in their length. It is their power and wayward temperament that are legend. Rainstorms can boost flow rates more than twenty-fold, bursting banks and pouring chaos onto surrounding lands. New channels are cut, earthworks ploughed and silt beds dumped, sometimes overnight.

As agents of change, rivers also operate on slower and grander timescales. Even during normal flow, currents bear waterborne silts and sands that wear away stone almost imperceptibly. Constancy of purpose will rout rock gorges, and in the case of rivers such as the Manawatu and Buller, breach whole mountain ranges. Both of these rivers have held their course for millions of years, since a time when the landscape was much flatter. As the present mountains were raised so they cut down through the land to keep pace with the rate of uplift, refusing to be budged by the forces of plate tectonics.

If rivers destroy landforms, they also create them. The proceeds of erosion picked up at one point are deposited elsewhere, laying down such fine works as swamps, riverflats and fertile terraces. Even on torn banks and scoured washouts, nature is quick to cloak past impropriety with regenerating vegetation. Life is more resilient than land. It adopts and adapts in the wake of change. In fact, the pioneer plants that spring up at the water's edge provide a habitat distinct from the more stable communities beyond the capricious reach of the river. Tangled *Muehlenbeckia* vines are a nursery for boulder copper butterflies, which lay their eggs on the foliage. Likewise, nettles on fresh slips lure red admiral butterflies which, by dint of precise flying, attach eggs onto the stinging hairs. Riverside scrub and open sunny ground favour geckos and skinks. There are also creatures here whose lives depend directly on the flowing water. Water spiders lurk by shoreside stones and mayflies launch from hiding with glittering flight.

Beneath the surface of the river, survival is perhaps more of a challenge. Here organisms must contend with the constant scouring of water. At first sight they would seem to have despaired, for most riverbeds appear as barren as deserts. Turn over a small boulder, however, and life is revealed beneath. Dozens of mayfly larvae wriggle away like miniature salamanders, and crayfish explode from their hideouts, tails flapping at the water with whip-cracks. Among major insect groups here — mayflies, caddisflies and stoneflies — specialists have identified almost 400 species, with more being added to the list each year. For most of us, though, the life of the river remains an unknown world. Aquatic animals are generally cryptic as well as nocturnal. Such is the case, too, for most of the thirty or so native fish, including that legendary inhabitant of the river depths, the eel.

This secretive world has become elegantly tuned to the demands of fast-flowing water. A close look at aquatic insect larvae will reveal many bearing exquisite tufts shaped like feathers or lace fans that sieve oxygen from the water. Many also have flattened bodies and hooked feet to crawl in the thin layer of relatively still water that exists close to the surface of rocks. Other animals, such as the larvae of sandflies, glue themselves down with pads of silk, playing out safety lines if they wish to move around. Silk is even more ingeniously used by some caddisfly larvae. They weave seine nets, strung between rocks to catch their food from the current.

Such sophistication extends to the senses that many aquatic creatures use to percieve their environment. There are stories of eels wriggling purposefully overland through damp vegetation, attracted somehow by the presence of an isolated body of water. More famous is the salmon's ability to return from the open ocean to the exact river tributary where it hatched. This it does by homing in on the particular chemical cues of its natal water, even when that water has been diluted a million-fold on its journey to the sea. But such talent bears a price in the modern world. The sensitivity of aquatic life to its environment is tied to an intolerance of pollution. It is a salient fact of nature that even water deemed pure enough for human consumption can be fatal to river animals.

Perhaps the most visually beautiful expression of river-sense is displayed by the blue duck. Inhabiting only the most pristine of forested waterways, the bird reads the surface currents and eddies with innate skill, to feed on aquatic larvae plucked from the riverbed. Usually active at dusk, it glides across tumbling water as if on a cushion of air, occasionally diving to grasp the bottom with its feet while it pecks for food. To scientists, the blue duck is an enigma. Very few ducks worldwide have adapted to life on fast-flowing rivers, and the blue duck, it seems, has no close relatives elsewhere. Like the kakapo and kokako, this bird is part of the unique biological identity of New Zealand.

Both the blue duck and its river habitat have suffered since human settlement. The clearance of forests and introduction of foreign plants and animals have transformed New Zealand's once widespread sylvan waterways, altering their food chains and physical environments. The impact on native life has been sometimes traumatic, and ended in extinction for a fish called the grayling. Once considered common and one of the most beautiful fish in New Zealand, the grayling vanished early this century. Its demise was so swift that there was not even the opportunity to identify the reasons. Habitat modification and trout introduction have both been implicated.

The depletion of aquatic habitats may continue, given the complex web of issues that confronts attempts to safeguard their natural values. Some waterways earn protection 'second-hand' by virtue of their flowing through national parks or reserves. But outside these boundaries, rivers are answerable to a multiplicity of demands. The problem is that where a farmer sees irrigation water, an angler sees the promise of trout; where a canoeist sees white water, a power board sees electricity generation; where a naturalist sees a wildlife refuge, industry sees waste-water disposal. Not least among such views are cultural values, of particular importance to Maori, who see in rivers a continuity of human experience with the landscape. The answers to these problematic issues are reached through compromise and principles of multi-use. But the question that worries conservationists is how much compromise can aquatic ecosytems accommodate. Also troubling is the fact that native aquatic animals and plants do not readily win advocates. Remote from our everyday existence, they do not rank alongside kokako and kauri trees in the human conscience. Efforts that have been made to protect river habitats have usually been for the sake of introduced sport fish.

Of all New Zealand's riverine habitats, none is more expansive in scale than the braided systems flowing east from the Southern Alps. Frost-shattered debris from the Ice Age fills the valley floors with wide shingle beds, across which powerful rivers spread silver skeins. Rivers here have room to play. They constantly shuffle their braids, each year weaving new paths between the mountain walls of the Main Divide.

These open valleys are hostile places. Winter snowfalls, spring floods and summer gales are keynotes of the seasonal cycle. But this austerity lends significance to what survives here. Crossing the desert of stones, one is drawn by the fragile but resolute evidence of life. Fine threads of silk left by a spider gleam with crystal brightness. Mauve flowers of *Wahlenbergia* nod among lichen-encrusted boulders. In springtime, migrant birds enter the scene. Dotterels, stilts and terns arrive from their coastal feeding grounds, intent on scraping a nest among the stones. You are likely to be greeted by the clamour of paradise shelducks, disturbed from their rest by your intrusion, or by the sound of Canada geese echoing from the valley walls. The activity is ardent and unexpected — a scene of life staking a claim in the barrens.

Among the nesting migrants is a fist-sized bird, the wrybill, that flies here from estuaries in the warm north of the country. Out on the riverbed, the wrybill sits discreetly. Only at the last moment of your approach will it rise from the rocks, feigning a broken wing to lure you from the eggs lying vulnerable on the ground.

Of all the river birds that were photographed for this book, the wrybill is the one I remember best. Lying eye to eye with the tiny bird, I was struck by its innate purpose. Upon its eggs, it sat at the centre of a universe, composed and alert to the world revolving around it. At times it would turn its gaze to intercept the sound of terns overhead, its eye an inquisitive window to the sky. If black-backed gulls flew near, it crouched protectively over its clutch, attempting to melt into the rocks.

I was struck, too, by the exquisite lateral curve of its beak, so perfect to probe beneath stones, and by the way its plumage toned so closely with the native greywacke rock. Both features were probably shaped by events intiated in the Pleistocene, when glaciers surged and retreated, laying down these stony beds to which the wrybill adapted. It took no leap of imagination to see this bird as part of the earth where it sat. So poised within its habitat, the wrybill possessed something that we in our increasingly urbanised society seem sorely to miss, a pure sense of belonging.

Time, however, could be running out for the wrybill. A threat has entered its life that is more pervasive than the prospect of flash floods, and swifter than the passage of glacial periods. Introduced plants, especially Russell lupins and willows, are changing the bird's nesting habitat. The plants are adept colonisers of the open riverflats, and each season witnesses fewer nest sites and more cover for introduced predators such as rats, cats and stoats. Even the very nature of the braided river system is under threat, for as the banks become stabilised by vegetation, so the rivers are locked in their paths rather than spreading across multiple channels.

If it is to survive in a human-modified world, the wrybill needs ongoing help. But one can question whether this will be forthcoming, given the current notion that everything should pay for itself. The wrybill is not likely to hold a cure for cancer, nor would its passing affect any other obvious ill that concerns people. But why should it be insisted that nature owes us something? The argument is based on human convenience. Nature, of course, owes us nothing. Rather, the reverse is true.

Attempts are underway, on behalf of the wrybill and other river birds, to restore some parts of their nesting habitat. Heavy machinery is at work in the upper Waitaki, uprooting willows and returning riverbeds as much as possible to their natural state. Taken alone, this may seem no more than a gesture, but the clanking of technology in deference to the needs of a small bird sounds a shift in attitude towards recognising the intrinsic worth of species. It is a small part in the realignment of western tradition, from that of consumer of the environment to custodian, exercising a role within, rather than over, nature. And if in future years the question is still asked, 'What is in it for us?', we may find the answer to be something closer to the human spirit than financial gain. Only by accepting the need for reciprocity in dealing with the landscape, and by more closely identifying with its living web, are we likely to reclaim our own sense of belonging.

AMONG THE WADERS returning each spring to nest on inland riverbeds of the South Island is the wrybill (*Anarhynchus frontalis*). It winters over in the North Island, feeding in coastal estuaries. The wrybill is endemic to New Zealand and unique because it has a lateral bend to its bill, thought to enable the bird to probe beneath rocks for insects and other invertebrates.

▲

A SMALL STREAM FLOWS
beneath the boughs of
mixed podocarp forest.
This is the archetypal
stream habitat, with clear
water running over a
stony bottom and much
of the food source for its

inhabitants being leaves
that fall from the canopy
above.

LOWLAND RIVER VALLEYS ▶
ring with the sound of
bird call. Among the
most eloquent of
songsters is the tui
(*Prosthemadera
novaeseelandiae*), perched
here on a miro branch.

NUDGED BY A PUFF OF breeze, spores spill from the capsule of a hair-cap moss (*Polytrichum*). Mosses are only partly adapted to life on land and so are most common in moist areas such as along stream banks and wet seepages. Most mosses lack a waterproof coating, or cuticle, which other land plants rely on to reduce desiccation, and they do not possess proper roots. They also require water during sexual reproduction, for mosses produce swimming sperm that need a film of moisture to travel through to reach the egg.

A SMALL FOREST STREAM spills over boulders. Continual tumbling produces richly oxygenated water, suited to the many insect larvae that live sheltered on the underside of submerged rocks. The steady shedding of leaves from the forest canopy provides organic matter upon which many of these larvae feed, laying the foundations of the food web for the stream life.

STONEFLY LARVAE
(Order Plecoptera) are
common river-bottom
dwellers, where they feed
on decaying vegetation,
or, in the case of some
species, on other insect
larvae. They have
flattened bodies and
widely splayed legs with
hooked feet, allowing
them to crawl around
without being swept away
by the current.

BROWN TROUT
(*Salmo trutta*) spawn in
the headwaters of rivers
in summer. During early
life, young fish such as
this one live in shallow
fast-moving water,
remaining near the
bottom and feeding on
insect larvae. When big
enough to compete with
other large trout, they
move into deep river
pools and become
territorial.

FRESHWATER CRAYFISH are common in rivers, as well as in swamps and lakes. There are two species. This one, *Paranephrops planifrons*, lives in the North Island. They shelter by day beneath rocks or in sediments on the bottom, emerging at night to scavenge for food. Freshwater crayfish are in turn an important food source for other animals, such as shags.

◀ AFTER SPENDING ITS larval life in a pond or wetland, the adult *Procordulia grayi* may venture widely in search of insects, often hawking the banks of rivers. Dragonflies are fast fliers and can control their flight by changing the frequency and amplitude of their wing beats, as well as the difference in phase between their front and rear wing pairs.

WITH DISTINCTIVE feathery fronds, the Prince of Wales fern (*Leptopteris superba*) is an aristocrat among ferns. It lives only in the dampest of situations and is exceedingly difficult to cultivate. These ferns are growing in sphagnum moss near a small forest stream. ▶

▲

A YOUNG BLUE DUCK (*Hymenolaimus malacoryhynchos*) preens itself by the riverbank. Blue ducks pair for life and claim a kilometre or two of river as their own, where they feed on aquatic insect larvae. Once fledged, juveniles such as this bird are encouraged to seek their fortunes elsewhere in the watershed.

A BLUE DUCK PERCHES ON a rock in the Oparara River, which flows through remote country near Karamea. This endemic bird, one of the few duck species world-wide to have adapted to life in fast-flowing rivers, is today found only in the most pristine of water-sheds. Once common throughout the country, blue ducks have faced both habitat loss and introduced predators. ▶

STILL DEPENDENT ON their egg-yolks for nutrition, Quinnat salmon (*Oncorhynchus tshawytscha*) begin life in the river headwaters. Ahead of them lies an epic of migration. As the fish grow they move downstream and enter the sea where they live for several years and grow to maturity. Then the fish return, and, relying on an extraordinary sense of scent for their birth-river, make their way back to the same tributary where they hatched. Here the females shed eggs in the gravel bed to be fertilised by the male, thus renewing the life cycle.

THE SCRUB THAT colonises old riverbeds and slips provides an ideal habitat for geckos. Here they feed on insects, nectar and the berries produced by many of the shrubs. This gecko, *Naultinus grayi*, lives in the north of the North Island.

THE WHIRINAKI RIVER plunges between bush-clad slopes in the central North Island. Rugged terrain has preserved this part of New Zealand as a showcase of pristine forested watersheds. It is a major North Island stronghold for the blue duck.

A BELLBIRD
(*Anthornis melanura*)
alights on a totara
branch. Birdlife is often
richest near rivers, where
fertile alluvial soils
promote forest growth.
Bellbirds dine on a
seasonal menu of berries,
nectar and insects, all of
which are in abundance
in lowland river valleys.

THE FIRST SIGHT OF mayflies (Order Ephemeroptera) on the wing is a promise that spring has started. The larvae live underwater, feeding on the river bottom, and emerge as adults during warming weather to gather in mating swarms. There is some urgency to court-ship, for mayfly adults cannot feed and are very short lived, some species surviving for only a matter of hours.

PHOTOGRAPHED AFTER sunset, the Waikato River funnels through a narrow gorge before plunging over the Huka Falls.

OPEN STONY RIVERBEDS have been colonised by a number of introduced plants brought by settlers. Among these is the sweet briar (*Rosa rubiginosa*).

THE NATIVE HUNTING wasp (*Priocnemis conformis*) makes short flights across the forest floor, constantly alighting to hunt for small species of spider, such as the trap-door spiders, often found near riverbanks. The reaction of the spider to the wasp can be described only as one of sheer terror. Some feign death while others flee, for once caught they are paralysed and used as a food source for the larvae of the wasp.

UNLIKE INTRODUCED frogs, the native Hamilton's frog (*Leiopelma hamiltoni*) does not depend on free water to raise its young and so is not restricted to ponds and wetlands. The eggs are laid on moist ground or wet mossy seepages and the tadpoles go through much of their early development while still enclosed by the egg membrane, hatching as tailed froglets. The male guards the eggs during this stage, and the hatched young crawl onto his moist body to continue their development.

THE INLAND RIVER BASINS of the Mackenzie Country are home to the endemic black stilt (*Himantopus novaezelandiae*). Here it wades the shallows, probing gravelly bottoms and silt beds for insect larvae, worms and other invertebrates. The species was once much more common, but habitat loss and introduced predators have pushed it close to extinction, with fewer than twenty breeding pairs left in the wild. Pure-bred black stilts are also vanishing because of interbreeding with the related pied stilt, which has become numerous since European settlement.

FREEZING FOGS HANG IN Mackenzie river basins for weeks at a time during spells of calm winter weather, casting a coat of hoar-frost over everything. The scene here is reminiscent of an English landscape, largely because of the introduced willows lining the riverbanks. Because of their propensity to colonise gravel riverbeds, willows have caused problems by smothering the open habitat needed for nesting black stilts, wrybills and other waders.

ON WARM SUNNY DAYS, jumping spiders are often out exploring stony riverbeds in search of insects. With keen eyesight and a powerful leap, they stalk and pounce upon their prey. Obstacles such as a gap between rocks are easily jumped. Upon reaching one side of the chasm the spider gauges the distance to the other side. The jump is exceedingly fast, being motivated by hydraulic pressure rather than by direct muscle action. A safety line is extruded during the leap, allowing the spider to return to its starting point just in case it fails to reach the target.

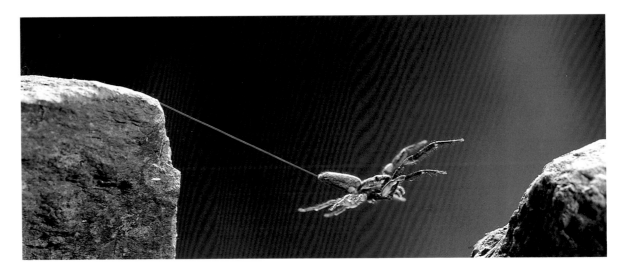

As it heads down from the mountains, the Waimakariri River forms braided channels across broad shingle flats. This is typical of many of the rivers of the eastern South Island, where rocky debris resulting from ice age erosion and subsequent frost shattering fills the valley floors. In spring these valleys are important nesting habitats for visiting lowland waterbirds.

◄ THE RED ADMIRAL butterfly (*Bassaris gonerilla*) is on the wing throughout summer and autumn, often near rivers, especially where slips have been colonised by stinging nettles. Female red admirals lay their eggs on the nettles, managing to place each egg on a stinging hair. Later the caterpillars browse the leaves, undeterred by the plant's defence.

▲ THE COMMON RIVER galaxias (*Galaxias vulgaris*) is typically a fish of fast-flowing inland rivers, where it feeds on small aquatic animals. It is a member of the Galaxiidae family, which is distributed widely in temperate regions of the southern hemisphere.

Kahikatea forest
fringes Arahaki Lagoon
in the central North
Island. The scene is
reminiscent of a time
millions of years ago
when New Zealand was
less mountainous and
swamp forests such as this
were extensive. In fact,
fossil records suggest the
kahikatea has changed
little since dinosaurs
roamed the earth.

THE WETLANDS

$\mathcal{H}$ISTORY HAS BEEN AN UNKIND JUDGE of wetlands. Swamp, bog and mire are words that have long been considered synonymous with wasteland, disease and decay. The opinion is as old as civilisation and the response has been single-minded — to drain and tame; to evict the smells, the uncertainty and the dampness.

Today we live in increasingly enlightened times, and attitudes to the world's wet places are changing, perhaps spurred by the lamentable truth that they have become so diminished. Wetlands are now seen to offer benefit to humankind. They moderate the boom and bust of the hydrological cycle and maintain water quality. Like large sponges they store water during heavy rainfall, so minimising flood damage downstream. The water is, instead, released slowly, maintaining river flows in times of low rainfall, so alleviating drought. At the same time wetlands act as vast filters, benefiting water quality by removing sediments and pollutants. In summary, wetlands are buffer zones, protecting their surroundings from environmental extremes.

Standing by the margins of a wetland, however, such concepts as buffer zones and hydrological cycles are somehow far removed and intangible. One contemplates, instead, the reality at hand. Ranks of reeds, rushes and other plants stretch away in an organic thatch of leaf-greens and ochreous browns, broken here and there by limpid pools of amber water. The seemingly impenetrable scene, combined with the soft and unpredictable ground underfoot, gives wetlands a secretive quality. They are wildernesses on a small scale, as aloof and unyielding to human intrusion as the remotest of mountain ranges.

What impresses most, however, is the life of these places. Contrary to their image as wasteland, wetlands nurture a wealth of wildlife. Nevertheless, do not expect easy sightings. The hurried visitor will find this landscape apparently untenanted, its inhabitants having gone to ground. You may only encounter the rustle of a coot as it evaporates in to the rushes, or the sudden rush of a duck disturbed from rest. Wetlands yield best to gentle enquiry, and it is more rewarding to listen than look. Sit quiet and tune into the conversation of unseen mallards, or hear the soft rhythmic calls of shovellers. Swallows catch insects from near the water's surface with an audible snap of the beak. Other sounds border on the subliminal. The metallic squeaks of fernbirds go unnoticed unless the mind is focused on them. Try tapping two rocks together and they will answer back, moving like ghosts through the foliage until they appear quite suddenly at arm's length. Sit long enough and you are aware of yet another sound, the background hum of droning insect wings and wind rustling through leaves. As the orchestration swells around you, it spells its message clear and simple — that nature here fulfils its imperative of diversity and multiplicity.

It is not only the life of wetlands that is enigmatic. These places also defy simple definition. The term wetland embraces habitats that range from shallow lakes through tussock and scrub to forested borders, where lofty stands of kahikatea and pukatea gain mushy footing on soft ground. It is hard to know where the wetland finishes and the land begins. The key, however, is water, which is present in such quantities that it demands special adaptations on the part of some inhabitants. As examples can be cited the spreading buttress roots of kahikatea used for support on the sagging earth, or the hollow breathing stems of the native sedge *Eleocharis*. Among animal specialists is the mudfish which, as pools seasonally dry up, burrows a refuge in the muddy bottom. Here it lies in a dormant state called aestivation, absorbing oxygen directly through its damp skin, and waiting until rains flood life back into its habitat.

The mosaic of wetland vegetation, from forest and scrub to reedbed and open water, is what sustains the diversity of wildlife. Moreover, wetlands are full of activity the year round. In winter, when most other landscapes fall quiet, tumultuous gatherings of waterfowl crowd water surfaces. Drakes, radiant in breeding plumage, vie like strutting prima donnas for the attention of females. Endless slap-water flights and petulant head-bobbing ceremonies punctuate the cool months. By spring, when the waterfowl have retreated to nest, dragonflies and damselflies trace whirling arabesques over the open water. Swamp grasses unfold pale green leaves and small insects drift through the air. Life animates this land- and waterscape. Swallows, starlings and fernbirds tumble, turn and snatch from the bounty. Summer nights pulse with the chorus of frogs.

As always, the food chain has its top carnivore. Here it is the harrier. There seems a nonchalance in this bird's spiralling flight, but the silhouette of its outstretched wings raises a furore among nesting birds below. Pied stilts and spur-winged plovers rise to intercept the threat, yapping and wheeling in the air, then fall like leaves to their eggs among the grass. If the agitated demeanour of the nesting birds is sufficient, the harrier will move on to search for easier pickings. If it finds an untended nest, the harrier will attack.

Attack, however, is perhaps the wrong word to use, with its connotation of wanton violence. The harrier does not know violence as we might define it. It is fulfilling its genetic imperative. The tendency to pin human motives and morals on animals is a way of thinking that sometimes influences our dealings with nature. Accordingly, the harrier earns indignation for killing other animals, and perhaps worse, for eating the flesh of dead carcasses. In the popularity stakes, mammals and birds are generally considered good and worthy, while fish, insects, snails and other creatures that slither or crawl count for little. Thus, while wetland visitors are quick to urge protection for the white heron, few have similar sympathy for the plight of threatened mudfish.

These values, rooted as they are in human morals rather than in biology, are no basis for making sound management decisions for a wetland, or any other habitat. At worst they engender a theme-park mentality in which the feathered are given precedence over the scaly and the instant appeal of alpine grandeur wins over the more subtle beauty of wetlands. The end result, ironically, becomes a projection of our own estrangement from nature, rather than an example of the true complexities of the living world. The reality is that each organism is a product of its neighbours, 'worthy' or otherwise. It is interrelationships, such as plant-pollinator and predator-prey, that bind ecosystems. One cannot favour the few without unhinging the whole.

Science has prescribed a more objective basis for dealing with nature. But it would be arrogant to assume that science alone can define nature. There are difficulties, for example, in applying human rationale to the study of animals, which live in a non-human world. Also, animal behaviour can be idiosyncratic and linked inextricably to the complex cues of the surrounding environment. We have trouble even understanding our own perceptions of the natural world. Who can really explain the awe inherent in the sight of geese flying across the evening sky, or the feelings of being dwarfed by thousand-year-old kahikatea trees rising from a swamp? These experiences are intangible, yet so vividly felt.

A plant, an animal, or an ecosystem is greater than the sum of all facts known about it. To contemplate the natural world fully is to realise that it is both tangible and intangible, factual and inexplicably mysterious. It inspires the artist as much as the scientist, feeding the imagination and curiosity of the human mind in ways that urban landscapes can never do. Within our desire to observe and seek meaning in the natural world lies much of the truth of what it means to be human. The corollary of this is that we cannot lose part of nature without also losing part of ourselves.

Wetlands worldwide have shrunk before the onrush of human ambition. In New Zealand, almost 90 percent of the habitat has vanished, most of it beneath grazing pastures. The trend, however, has not all been one-way. Wetlands are relatively easy to re-create in comparison with other habitats. I know of one family who retired 60 hectares of their peatlands farm. They dammed part of its drainage and then watched as land once destined for sheep turned to fernbird scrub, open water, and home to some 2000 waterfowl.

This is not an isolated incident. It has happened in a small way on farms and Crown land over the length of the country. Some people have done it to provide duck-shooting habitat. Others are less clear of their motives. Perhaps it is the joy of being close to wildlife, or of watching the changing seasons. The reasons are not easily explained, nor do they need to be. Those who become captivated by wetlands find it hard to imagine a world in which they no longer exist.

SCAUP (*Aythya novaeseelandiae*) belong to a group of ducks called diving ducks, that can submerge several metres to search the bottom for crustacea, molluscs and other invertebrates. For this reason they stay further from shore than other ducks, and are often seen on lakes gathered in rafts of a dozen or so birds. They swim underwater by paddling vigorously and have legs set back on their bodies to enhance diving efficiency. This makes them clumsy walkers on land, so they rarely come ashore.

IN CALM MOMENTS, WATER
has the ability to instil a
feeling of tranquillity.
Nowhere is this truer
than at places such as
Lake Paringa, where
pristine forests stretch to
the shore.

IN BREEDING PLUMAGE
the shoveller drake (*Anas rhynchotis*) is undoubtedly the most colourful of New Zealand's waterfowl. It may not always be noticed, however, for it is a shy bird staying close to cover. Often the only indication of its presence is the sound of its call, a softly repetitive 'choo-kook', floating out of the rushbeds. If disturbed at close quarters, the bird can put on an outstanding airborne escape, exploding almost vertically from the water and rocketing away at incredible speed.

GREEN CURTAINS OF *Weymouthia* moss drape everything in this swamp forest by the Moeraki River, producing the appearance of an underwater garden. In reality this is not far from the truth, for the moss thrives only in the dampest of situations, where it receives almost perpetual drenchings of mist or rain.

GEORGE CHANCE

SOON AFTER HATCHING, the cryptically patterned chicks of the crested grebe (*Podiceps cristatus*) scramble onto their parent's back for protection and warmth. Here they can be seen while the other parent returns offering a whitebait for food. Grebes belong to a very ancient line of birds that have existed since the time of the dinosaurs. They are expert divers, able to swim underwater with the aid of lobed toes and legs set well back under their tails. This makes them clumsy on land, so they spend virtually all their life on water.

LARGE LOWLAND LAKES with pristine forest margins have become rare since European settlement, but can still be found in South Westland. Along the shores of Lake Paringa there is an extremely swift transition from open water, through fringes of flax and jointed rush, to tall forest, and this provides microhabitats for numerous plants and animals. Here, during the misty quiet of early morning, you are likely to encounter waterfowl and forest birds such as tui and pigeons within metres of one another.

▲

AFTER DARK, A NATIVE leaf-veined slug (Arthorocophoridae Family) glides down a nikau frond. Moist-bodied creatures such as slugs are active at night to avoid dessication. By day they hide away and can often be found in the wet leaf bases of nikau palms or between flax leaves.

WITH LARGE FORWARD-facing eyes, the whistling frog (*Litoria ewingi*) gauges its trajectory before it leaps into the air. This now widespread, introduced Australian species, is a tree frog. Species of tree frog are found worldwide, with particularly colourful members in the Amazon rainforests. They all have suckered toes, allowing them to gain purchase on vegetation. ▶

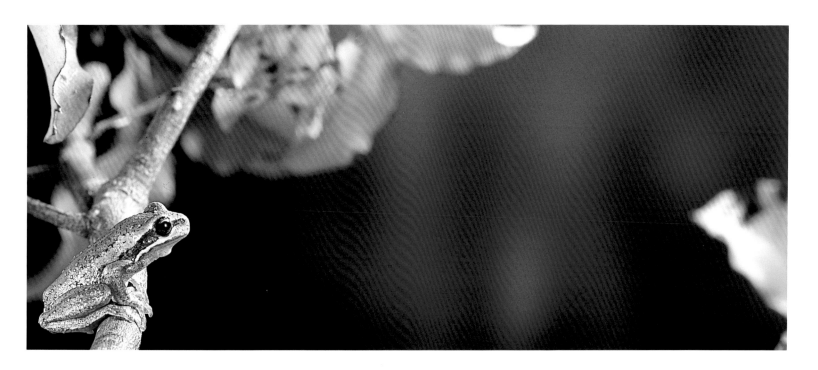

MAGNIFICENTLY buttressed trunks of kahikatea (*Dacrycarpus dacrydiodes*) rise from swamp water at Arahaki Lagoon in the central North Island. The buttresses help support the tree on soft ground. Kahikatea also has a shallow root system, which, when interlocked with neighbouring trees, becomes a living raft on the waterlogged soil.

KIDNEY FERNS (*Trichomanes reniforme*) and *Lycopodium volubile* sprawl across moist ground near a swamp. Both belong to primitive plant groups that produce free-swimming sperm during sexual reproduction, requiring water to complete their life cycle. Lycopodium often grows in more open scrubby areas, but kidney ferns are found only in moist forests, as their translucent leaves soon shrivel in the sun.

RELATIVELY RECENT immigrants from Australia, grey teal (*Anas gibberifrons*) are now established in New Zealand. They are dabbling ducks like the mallard and shoveller, but are much smaller and can also be distinguished by their crimson eyes. They nest close to water, preferably in a hollow tree trunk.

AFTER A DEWY NIGHT every small shrub in the wetland glitters with jewelled cobwebs. On such mornings it is startling to see how many spiders there are, and the diversity of homes they spin. Apart from orb webs such as this one, there are trapeze-like structures as well as the nests of the nurseryweb spider draped over the tops of branches like paper handkerchiefs.

A FEMALE MALLARD (*Anas platyrhynchos*) warily escorts her young on a foraging trip. Good winter rains have flooded the wetland margins, providing extensive feeding areas and enabling her to rear so many young. Mallards are dabbling ducks, feeding by tipping tail-up to dredge the shallows for submerged vegetation and invertebrates. Introduced from the northern hemisphere, they have become widespread and are interbreeding with the closely related native grey duck.

A GREEN TREE FROG (*Litoria raniformis*) loafs among the duckweed growing on a pond. Its large protruding eyes afford excellent vision, and if it senses danger, it will vanish beneath the water with a plop.

WAXEYES (*Zosterops lateralis*) can often be seen near lakes and along riverbanks where berries, nectar and insects are to be found. In spring, flocks are attracted to stands of kowhai flowering by the water's edge. Such groups are highly argumentative and have a strict pecking order, with individuals relying on body postures and aggressive displays to assert rank.

THE KOPUATAI PEAT Dome in the Waikato Valley is one of only three natural sanctuaries for the bamboo-like rush *Sporodanthus traversii*, growing here with manuka. About 10,000 hectares in extent, Kopuatai is the largest domed bog in natural state in New Zealand and is a key refuge for at least nine vulnerable or threatened plant and animal species.

THE NATIVE MILFOIL (*Myriophyllum robustum*) is one of New Zealand's threatened aquatic plants. Once widespread in the North and South Islands, it has suffered both habitat loss and competition from introduced plants. Today it is restricted to just a few sites, usually by lake margins and under kahikatea stands.

77

THE COLOURFUL AND noisy pukeko (*Porphyrio porphyrio*) is not typical of the rail family to which it belongs. Most rails are cryptic and take care not to attract attention to themselves in the swamp. Pukeko are nevertheless successful and have coped relatively well with habitat changes caused by humans. Though never far from the sanctuary of a swamp, they can often be seen strutting across nearby farmland, feeding on soft vegetation and insects such as grass grubs.

THE HARRIER (*Circus approximans*) is New Zealand's most common bird of prey. In spring it nests in dense swamp vegetation and scours the surrounding countryside for small game. Its whistling call and spiralling flight elicit attention from other nesting wetland birds, anxious to safeguard their own young. A harrier's plumage changes colour as it ages. Older birds such as this one have pale brown plumage, while younger birds are much darker in colour

AFTER MONTHS SPENT living underwater as a wingless larva, an adult blue damselfly (*Austrolestes colensonis*) has just emerged. During this transition from water to air the larva crawls from the pond by climbing vegetation and its case splits, allowing the adult to extract itself. The adult remains vulnerable until its soft body and wings have expanded and dried. Once the wings have hardened it will take its maiden flight and hunt for food nearby. Several days later, by which time it is ready to breed, the damselfly will have acquired its iridescent blue colouration.

THE BLUE DAMSELFLY spends its larval life underwater in the pond. Here it lives among the waterweeds, feeding on other small aquatic creatures it catches with an extendable lower lip called a mask. This is shot out by an hydraulic action at lightning speed to grasp the prey firmly.

On a warm summer's day the airspace near ponds and wetlands will glitter with the courtship dances of damselflies. Males of the blue damselfly set up territories around clumps of grasses and perch in the centre. Females entering the claimed airspace are pursued for mating. But when a rival male encroaches, as seen here, disputes can escalate into mid-air battles, with one attempting to ram the other and drive it away.

CREEPING GUNNERA
(*Gunnera prorepens*) can
be found in bogs from the
Waikato to Stewart
Island, from sea level to
the alpine zone. The
cheerful raspberry-like
fruit are formed in
autumn.

Astelia fragrans GROWS BY the dark, peat-stained waters of a swamp stream. There are thirteen species of *Astelia* in New Zealand, ranging from those with large flax-like leaves to turf-forming alpine species with leaves no larger than matchsticks. Many of these species favour wet ground.

DISCARDED DURING THE moult, a paradise shelduck feather has been left stranded on some rushes by the water's edge.

THE PIED STILT (*Himantopus himantopus*) is one of the most familiar of wetland birds, although it has only become widespread since European settlement. Stilts can be seen on coastal mudflats, lake margins and damp paddocks, wading with their very long legs and plucking a diet of small invertebrates from the water.

THE UBIQUITOUS
starling (*Sturnus vulgaris*)
is common in wetlands
and damp paddocks
where it feeds on insects
and other invertebrates.
The birds nest in hollow
tree trunks, or failing

that, any dark enclosed
space. This bird is
emerging from its nest-
hole in the wall of a
derelict farmhouse. The
parents constantly ferry
food to their growing
chicks, and since what

goes in must come out,
they also have to carry
out the droppings.

THE BLUE DAMSELFLY (*Austrolestes colensonis*) is the largest and most striking native damselfly. It is seen near most ponds, floating through the air with glittering wings and flashes of iridescent blue. Large spherical eyes provide an outstanding field of vision, allowing it to hover among the rushes and successfully hunt for craneflies, mosquitoes and other small prey.

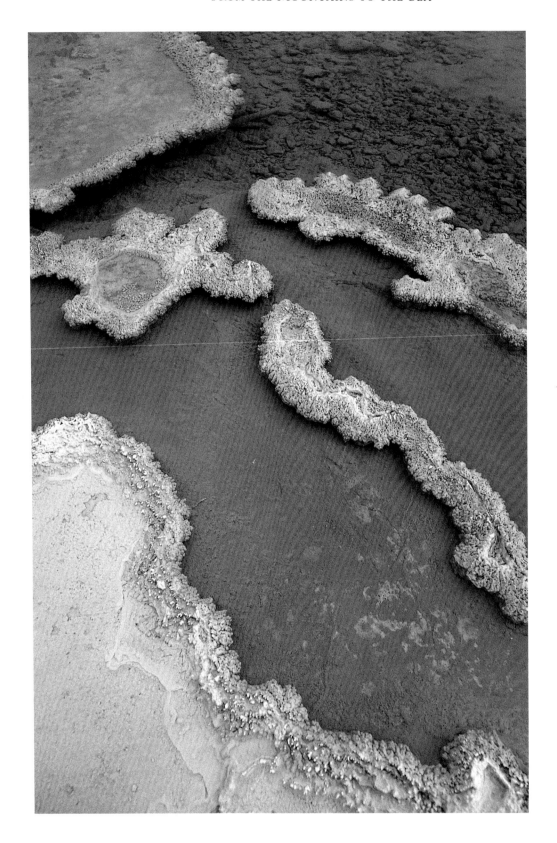

SCALDING TEMPERATURES, extremes of pH and high concentrations of mineral salts are typical of thermal pools such as the Champagne Pools (opposite) and the Inferno Crater (above) at Rotorua. Yet there are groups of simple bacteria living in these conditions, even in water close to boiling. Biotechnologists are keenly interested in these organisms and the methods by which they survive. Some have been discovered to produce compounds useful for industrial high-temperature chemical processing.

GEORGE CHANCE

THE AUSTRALIAN LITTLE grebe (*Tachybaptus novaehollandiae*) is one of the rarest and most striking of wetland birds. Individuals probably arrived in New Zealand in the late 1960s as stragglers from Australia, and have colonised a few small lakes and lagoons. They are quiet, secretive birds, often only being given away by their trilling call. Grebes build a floating nest amongst emergent water plants in the shallows.

90

CAUGHT MID-WAY through executing a left-hand turn, this redcoat damselfly (*Xanthocnemis zealandica*) demonstrates its aerial agility. With two wing pairs that move out of phase, damselflies can perform wonderfully precise manoeuvres. Hovering, for example, is accomplished by counterstroking the wings in a horizontal plane, very much like helicopter blades. This flying ability, combined with superb eyesight, has contributed to the modern-day success of damselflies, despite belonging to one of the most primitive orders of winged insects.

WITH A FINAL TURN, A small creek empties into the Tasman Sea. Here at the juncture of river and ocean is the meeting of two water worlds. In spring, shoals of whitebait migrate from saltwater to freshwater and head upstream to grow to adulthood. In most areas, however, large runs have become a thing of the past. Inland modification of rivers and wetlands has left sparingly little habitat suitable for the fish.

RETURN TO THE SEA

AUTUMN SHOWERS, SUNLIGHT ON SNOW, grass laden with dew: a river near journey's end is the distillation of countless origins. It travels ever more slowly across the final kilometres, as if hesitant to yield history to the ocean. Waterplants sway in idle backcurrents and small animals — diving beetles, water boatmen and shrimps — ply the calm. Here and there, blooms of algae tint the surface a lustrous green, like the patina on polished jade.

When it finally reaches the estuary, the river comes under the influence of the sea. The movement of water is halted and reversed twice each day by the incoming tide, and this hesitation causes wide flats of fine mud and silt to be deposited. Here, as is often the case at the boundary between two environments, there is an outstanding richness of life. Wander over the flats at low tide and you will encounter the serpentine castings of burrowing worms and the meandering trails of mud snails. Thousands of mud crabs watch you with eyes on stalks, and vanish down their burrows with a faint popping sound. And when the tide returns, fish and transparent shrimps glide over the submerged plains to feed. Deeper down, concealed within the mud itself, beds of shellfish and numerous species of bristleworm and polychaete worm sift specks of organic food from the ooze and overlying water.

Biologists calculate that in terms of their living mass, estuaries are more productive than most agricultural lands. The continual input of organic debris and nutrient-rich sediments from river and sea attend to this, fostering the growth of algae and other plants on which the estuarine community depends. If you ever doubt the fecundity of this habitat when viewing the seemingly bleak plains of black mud exposed by the outgoing tide, you only need to watch the troops of stilt-legged birds that pick their way across the flats. Long bills, working like forceps, pluck out the hidden bounty. Cockles, worms and tiny crustacea are extracted and dispatched by the dozen.

At larger estuarine areas, such as Miranda in the Firth of Thames, upwards of 50,000 wading birds gather during the summer season. At high tide a flock will often take wing and move in swirls like giant snowflakes caught in some invisible vortex. The air roars through thousands of wings and then the group drops silently to earth, settling with the coordinated grace of a single organism. If these congregations are studied in more detail, they reveal themselves to be a varied and multinational company. Among them are resident New Zealanders, such as oystercatchers and wrybills, which migrate inland to nest each spring. Other waders — the godwits, knots, sandpipers and turnstones — are truly cosmopolitan. Come the lengthening shadows of autumn, they swap these coastal saltmarshes for their nesting grounds among the muskeg and cottongrass meadows of the Arctic, half a world away.

The impulse that drives some birds to migrate across ocean and continent has long fascinated humans. Weeks after its departure, a godwit may be in Alaska, replenishing its fat reserves on the insect life that thrives in the Arctic spring. Its journey would have been conducted in stages, some of considerable length. Knots are thought to travel distances measuring several thousand kilometres non-stop. Such endurance in so slight an animal is almost beyond human imagining. The intent and navigation is worth contemplating while watching the flocks feeding on the mudflats. Wading on thousands of reedy legs is a collective knowledge that would fill volumes; an intuitive understanding of the language of wind, sea and star, instilled by millions of years of evolution.

The estuary is as vital to the life cycle of many fish as it is to wading birds. Some marine species congregate in estuaries and rivermouths to spawn, the freshwater probably acting as a beacon to draw breeding individuals together. Other fish rely on estuaries as nurseries. Among these are flounder and sole, which often spend their early lives here, growing quickly in these fertile feeding grounds before heading further out to sea.

For several species of river fish the estuary is a crossroads. In autumn, freshwater eels pass this way on a seawards migration to their spawning grounds in the Pacific. After many years spent growing to adulthood in the river headwaters, they cease feeding and their eyes become enlarged in preparation for a long journey through the twilight depths of the ocean. Exactly where they go to spawn, or indeed, how they find their way is not known. But succeed they must, for each spring a new generation of transparent eel larvae finds its way to the estuary and heads up-river to grow to maturity.

Shoals of whitebait, the young of native galaxiid fish, also pass through the estuary at this time, heading up-river to grow into adults. Their story began the preceeding autumn, when parent fish travelled down-river to the estuary to spawn. The adults time their arrival to coincide with the night of the full or new moon, for this is when high spring tides flood the estuary margins. Swimming across submerged saltmarshes, the adults shed eggs and milt, which are left stranded for two weeks while the smaller neap tides come and go. Then when the next spring tides submerge the eggs, they hatch and the minute fish larvae enter the sea where they grow to become whitebait.

This toing and froing between river and sea is no simple matter. For migratory fish, the estuary is a border between two worlds, one of saltwater and the other of fresh. Here they must spend time waiting 'in transit' while their bodies undergo the physiological changes that allow them to make the move between environments. Salmon returning from the sea to breed pause by the estuary mouth while they become accustomed to freshwater. The phenomenon is so entrenched in the salmon's life that some farmed species undergo it even in their fish pens. They cease swimming endless circuits of the tank perimeter and all face the same direction, towards an imagined river. Salmon farmers speak of the fish as 'watching TV'.

To become familiar with even a few of the interactions that make up an estuary is to appreciate that ecosystems are far more than conglomerations of plants and animals. It is not the individual organisms that are important so much as the relationships between them, and the relationships between the organisms and the land. These relationships give form and intent to all living things. They, for instance, link the length of a godwit's probing beak to the hidden life of a mud-worm, the dimensions of a small *Notoacmea* limpet to the width of the sea-grass leaves it grazes on, and the reproductive timing of galaxiid fish to the phases of the moon.

All species are the product of evolution — the process whereby organisms are shaped over successive generations by their interactions with one another and with the non-living components of their environment. To consider a species in isolation, outside the landscape that defines it, is as informative as a single word plucked from a story. Like the salmon that 'watches TV' in its pen, the complexities of purpose have become indecipherable. Only within the context of the ecosystem where it evolved can an organism express the fullness of its adaptation.

Nothing stands alone. Even the estuary cannot be treated as separate from the wider surrounds. Tamper with it and the repercussions spread, causing ripples in places that may at first seem too distant to bear relation, such as Arctic nesting grounds and spawning waters of the deep Pacific. Ecosystems, like species, are part of a larger story, bound by links often too subtle or complex to fathom easily.

Conservation, therefore, is not about protecting one animal here or another there. It is about protecting the integrity of nature, the myriad interactions that constitute the ongoing processes of natural creation. The common catchwords of conservation — save the whale, the kakapo, the hoiho, and so on — are valid expressions of compassion. But the hope of protecting what any organism 'really is' can only be fulfilled with the protection of the natural habitat where it evolved, and where it will continue to evolve. This, for conservationists, is often the most difficult challenge.

Without this habitat protection, however, little can be achieved. There can be no joy in saving relics of a system that is no longer functioning, and thus condemning species to lead their lives, half-eclipsed, in captivity. A whale without seas to roam wild in has been robbed of its ecological integrity. People who wonder at nature will agree, too, that the animal has been robbed of its aesthetic integrity.

The tendency for humans to settle coastlines has often compromised estuaries. Many of these tidal habitats have lost their thickly forested margins of tall podocarp trees, and some have been 'reclaimed' and encased in concrete for port facilities. But one can still find places where it is possible to wander the muddy margins, enthralled by the sight of wild birds flowing with the wind. Where interesting plant communities remain intact, interpretational walks have often been opened for those who care to see. Here I can think of walkways in Northland that explore trellised stands of mangroves, where school groups and adults can explore first hand the inter-relatedness and dynamics of nature.

I have visited, too, a small walkway at Okuru, deep in the heart of coastal South Westland. It winds between spires of rimu hung with kiekie vines and beneath a kowhai canopy that blazes with flowers in spring. At the lookout, where the river twists round to the ocean, you look across a profusion of floating plants, animated by fin and feather. It is a scene that you can turn from reassured, taking heart in the knowledge that there are places where nature is still in good health. For it is upon the health of the grand cycles of the global ecosystem that all life depends, not least our own.

THE WHITE-FACED HERON (*Ardea novaehollandiae*) is a patient hunter, quietly stalking the shallows and eyeing the bottom for food. It strikes, however, with lightning speed, uncoiling its neck to pluck out prey. This bird was feeding on mud crabs, swallowing them whole with a toss of the head. Large items can pose a problem for the heron, as it cannot tear them into bite-sized chunks. I watched this bird later catch a particularly big flounder, which it attempted to swallow for about twenty minutes, with as much luck as if it were trying to down a dinner-plate.

NEAR HAAST, ONSHORE winds combined with the steady uplift of plate tectonics have produced a system of raised sand dunes that parallel the coast. Older, inland dunes have become covered in forest and enclose finger-like lakes. In this photograph the sedge *Eleocharis sphacelata* that borders the lake is spreading slowly inwards, allowing organic matter and silts to accumulate in the shallow water between its stems. Other plants will colonise the lake as it fills, culminating after several centuries in tall forest.

THE RED PERCHER dragonfly (*Diplacodes bipunctata*) is the smallest of New Zealand's dragonflies, measuring about 30 mm in length. It is most common in the northern North Island and takes its name from the habit of perching discreetly on a suitable vantage point. From here it studies the movement of nearby objects, twisting its head to keep them in sight. It darts off with a burst of speed to pursue prey or to court females.

FLOCKS OF GODWITS (*Limosa lapponica*) wheel in the air at Miranda in the Firth of Thames. Miranda is a major feeding ground for waders, hosting more than 50,000 birds. Many of these, including godwits, are summer migrants that depart during autumn for their nesting grounds as far away as Siberia and Alaska.

100

WITH BILLS TUCKED under wings, pied oystercatchers (*Himantopus ostralegus*) wait out the high tide at roost. Once the retreating sea has exposed the mudflats, the birds will be able to disperse and feed. Despite their name, oystercatchers do not eat oysters, which live in water too deep for them to reach, but probe the mud for worms, crustacea and molluscs. In particular they are fond of cockles, splitting them open with a downwards thrust of their strong beak. A bird may eat over two hundred cockles in a day.

BARE SUNNY RIVERBANKS are a good place to look for native wasps and bees, which burrow tunnels here as a refuge for their larvae. The mason wasp (*Pison spinolae*), however, visits these sites to sunbathe and to collect pellets of soft earth to build its nest elsewhere. New Zealanders in warmer parts of the country will recognise these mud structures, which are often found around the home — in keyholes, the angles of joinery, or any suitable crevice. They consist of several mud cells, each containing a wasp larva and one or more paralysed spiders for food.

A GREEN SKINK (*Leiolopisma chloronotum*) hunts among the driftwood for small animals. Skinks can be found in open habitats from the alpine zone to the coast. Although termed cold blooded, they control their body temperature by basking. On sunny mornings you can sometimes spot them sitting quietly soaking up the warmth.

A WHITE-FACED HERON (*Ardea novaehollandiae*) demonstrates the meaning of the term 'to crane one's neck' as it checks out a potential threat some distance away.

WHERE THE RIVER crosses farmland, its banks are clothed in wildflowers. For farmers this is a source of weed seeds likely to infest their land, but for insects such as this bumblebee (*Bombus terrestris*), the unkempt vegetation offers a banquet of nectar and pollen.

THE BLACK SWAN (*Cygnus atratus*) is common in shallow coastal lakes, lagoons and estuaries, where it can reach the bottom with its long neck to graze on submerged vegetation. The nest is built close to the water's edge by heaping up nearby vegetation to form a mound. Swans pair for life and both parents share the tasks of raising a family.

ONLY ONE DAY OLD, a black swan cygnet sits by its nest. Once its siblings have hatched it will accompany its parents on to the water, feeding on aquatic plants and shoreside vegetation.

Young swans are relatively slow growing and usually do not fledge till they are more than three months old. Adults may live for over twenty years.

Although not uncommon overseas, the kotuku, or white heron (*Egretta alba*), is rare in New Zealand. There is just one nesting colony, situated in kahikatea forest bordering the Waitangiroto River near Okarito Lagoon. Nesting starts in spring, coinciding with the arrival of whitebait runs in the local rivers, and continues until about January when the birds disperse throughout the country. The long breeding plumage of the adults was once a desirable item in the fashion trade, and this led to the colony being depleted to just a handful of birds by about 1940. Since then, protection has witnessed a good recovery and numbers now exceed one hundred.

AT THE COASTAL LAGOON of Okarito, kotuku, or white herons, feed against a backdrop of Mount Cook and the Southern Alps. The herons disperse throughout New Zealand during autumn and winter, but return to Okarito during September in preparation for nesting nearby.

THE COMMON COPPER butterfly (*Lycaena salustius*) is often found near rivers and along coasts where species of *Muehlenbeckia* vine provide food for its caterpillars. This individual is shedding wing scales, having brushed against a glasswort stem, a common saltmarsh plant.

THE NATIVE COAST MUSK (*Mimulus repens*) is one of the prettiest flowering plants found in the saltmarsh, where it usually grows close to water. It is related to the larger yellow-flowered monkey musk, an introduced plant common on stream banks and damp road verges.

A MINIATURE GARDEN OF diverse mosses, ferns and grasses sprawls at the base of this kahikatea tree, where periodic tidal flooding from the nearby river has prevented the growth of larger, understorey plants. Some of the small plants have gained a relatively drier footing by perching on the root buttresses of the kahikatea.

MAGNIFICENT STANDS OF
rimu, entwined with
lianes, border a river
where it enters the sea.

BETWEEN DECEMBER AND July, wrybills (*Anarhynchus frontalis*) feed at estuaries and mudflats in the North Island, particularly in the Auckland area. In spring they migrate to nesting sites on the inland riverbeds of Otago and Canterbury.

WASHED OUT TO SEA from the forested hinterland, a piece of driftwood is cast up by the tide.

By THE RIVERMOUTH A young fur seal (*Arctocephalus forsteri*) appears to contemplate life in that other water realm, the ocean. Fur seals sometimes frequent major rivermouths, where sediments being washed out to sea nurture a rich food chain, attracting congregations of fish and other prey species.

PHOTOGRAPHIC NOTES

Equipment and film

It is people, not cameras, that take photographs. Camera manufacturers constantly extol the complex functions and features of their various models, but the critical requirements of any camera are that it be robust, easy to use and designed to allow control by the photographer rather than by on-board microprocessors.

For this book I used two Olympus camera bodies fitted with lenses ranging from 24 mm to 400 mm in focal length. The macro (close-up) studies of small subjects were done with 80 mm and 100 mm focal-length lenses, while most of the bird photography was done using a 400 mm focal-length lens. The landscapes, forest interiors and remaining photographs were taken with 24 mm, 50 mm and 100 mm focal-length lenses. With very few exceptions, tripods were used throughout. A Velbon Victory 550 tripod fulfilled most needs, being relatively light for carrying in the field, while at the same time being adjustable to cope with the most awkward of situations, including photography at near-ground level. Its only limit came with the large 400 mm lens, where a heavier and more solid tripod was preferable.

Fujichrome films have gained an increased following among outdoor photographers in recent years. The film stocks I used were Fujichrome Velvia and Fujichrome 100 D Professional.

Velvia has several qualities of benefit to nature work. Apart from being fine-grained, it is a film of choice when colour is important. It is well known for delivering saturated colours, but perhaps less widely appreciated for its ability to define subtle variances of colour hue. For example, where other films may register some of the different greens in a forest interior as tones, Velvia differentiates between these greens. Thus mosses, ferns, trees and other plants stand out from one another according to their intrinsic colours. Another asset of Velvia is its virtual immunity to reciprocity failure. This is a problem that plagues many films when shot at shutter speeds longer than one second, and manifests itself as an annoying shift in colour balance and a drift towards underexposure. Velvia's trueness to colour and exposure in these situations is invaluable for forest interior photography and macro work by natural light, where long exposures are mandatory.

All films, however, have idiosyncrasies. In Velvia's case this seems to be an intolerance of underexposure, which is best avoided by bracketing a series of exposures in dim or low-key light situations. There may also be times when the bold saturated colours that Velvia produces are not called for, and the photographer prefers more muted colours. In these cases it may pay to try another film, such as Kodachrome 64 or Fujichrome 50.

Fujichrome 100 D Professional film was used predominantly for wildlife photography with the 400 mm telephoto lens. Its greater light sensitivity compared with Velvia permitted faster shutter speeds, so minimising camera shake that is problematic with long telephotos. The film also has the bonus that its light sensitivity can be uprated even further, a feature I was grateful for when working in the dull light conditions of Fiordland. This allows the film to be shot at ASA settings of up to 400, so long as it is then push-processed to correct the exposure.

Techniques

When I first announced to some friends that I intended doing a book on rivers and wetlands, and that it would take a year of full-time photography to obtain the hundred or so photographs needed, they responded by asking what I was going to do for the rest of the year. I was to wonder at these words often over the ensuing months, because of course, there was never to be a 'rest of the year'. The key ingredient for nature photography is time, and I was to need every hour, every waking minute.

Nature shots often require days, if not weeks, of advance planning. This is particularly so for wildlife, as good results depend on an understanding of the subject as much as a knowledge of photography, and animals are considerably more complex than cameras. Tackling each species becomes a whole new learning experience. Aspects of the animal's behaviour, daily routine and living requirements may all need to be investigated before success can be achieved.

Birds require perhaps the most homework. Unfortunately, nature photographers do not possess miracle telephoto lenses, capable of rendering detailed close-ups from hundreds of metres away. The most powerful lens I used was a 400 mm, which meant a working distance of less than five metres for many of my subjects. This lies well within the 'flight-zone' of most birds, which, with gifted eyesight and nervous disposition, often flee before a human is within a hundred metres.

Getting close takes patience and subterfuge. Stalking is one method. The objective here is not to creep up without being seen (birds are far too astute for this), but to approach in a slow and unobtrusive manner so that they will tolerate your presence. The photographer wears 'quiet' earth colours and moves gradually closer to the bird, pretending all the while not to take any interest in it. This works for relatively tame species, such as blue ducks and oystercatchers, but most birds, especially those living in wetlands, are suspicious of anything unfamiliar. It is also well nigh impossible to be unobtrusive in a wetland, wading through dense vegetation and gurgling mud, with the prospect of vanishing at any instant into the mire.

Often, therefore, one resorts to using a hide, which is a tent-like structure in which the photographer can sit without being seen by the bird. The problem is that hide work is time consuming. Before one can be placed, the bird must be observed discreetly with binoculars, noting its daily routine and habits so as to work out which photographic site has the best chance of providing a close encounter. Examples include places where the bird regularly feeds or roosts. Nesting offers another, more obvious, opportunity; but, because of the possibilty of causing the bird major distress at a very vulnerable stage of its life cycle, this option should be the last chosen, if at all.

Each potential hide site must then be evaluated for its aesthetic potential, including the needs of composition and light. Comfort generally comes last on the list of considerations. The best photographs portray birds on their own terms, and for wetland birds this can mean the cold, damp reality of working part-submerged in water for many hours on end.

If being hide-bound for long hours in a swamp sounds like a form of self-torture, there are compensations. It never ceases to amaze me how much goes on in these places when you sit quiet and unseen. While working on pukeko I have been entertained by the airborne courtship dances of harriers. Mallards have swum by with feeding young in tow, filling my hide with the musical percussion of their snap-clapping beaks. I have watched pairs of white-faced heron prancing together in a seeming nuptial trance and observed stilts swooping so vigorously in territorial disputes that I could hear the wind roaring in their wings. Anyone who has studied nature will understand the thrill of seeing some animal at close quarters for the first time, or of witnessing some new aspect of behaviour. And nothing surpasses the final moment when the chosen subject steps out from the reeds, radiant and vital, to fill the viewfinder.

These, of course, are the good times. I would be romanticising the nature photographer's work if I did not also admit that there were failures. There was, for instance, the time I returned to one site after heavy rains to discover that the birds had vanished and so had the wetland. A flood had transformed the area into a lake, broken only by the forlorn sight of my hide, its top just poking above the lapping waves. Another time I had lured harriers to a photographic site over several days by using rabbit meat as bait. Then, on the appointed day when I lay in wait with my camera, the harrier landed, took a bored look at the rabbit offerings, and flew off never to be seen again, despite my waiting another twenty hours over the next three days. It turned out that the local rabbit-control board had had their annual shoot just the night before and all the harriers for far and wide had gorged themselves on rabbit.

Perhaps the most comical episode (at least in hindsight) was being dropped off by boat to look for blue ducks in the Fiordland wilderness. A heavy rain warning had been issued, and as I leapt ashore, the boat driver muttered something about floods on that particular stretch of river. That day I made several futile searches for ducks in the strengthening drizzle before returning, rather disconsolate, to my isolated bush camp. Here, getting damper as moisture inexorably seeped through the tent and into my sleeping bag, I found that the radio I needed to call up my return trip no longer seemed to work. This alarming discovery, however, was soon overshadowed by a sudden roaring of water as the river burst its banks and started to elbow into my campsite. Then, as sometimes happens in the midst of adversity, the situation descended into the absurd. Just as I was making an anxious evacuation to higher ground, a blue duck was swept around the corner, paddling so furiously to escape the current that it almost shot inside the tent. I do not know which of us was more surprised. One can only see the ridiculous irony of such situations, and reassure oneself that things can only get better. As it turned out, the weather in Fiordland cleared over the following days and I was able to find and photograph the duck to my heart's content.

Some of these problems are alleviated when working with small animals such as insects, which can be manipulated to a limited extent. Flying insects, however, pose a new set of difficulties that are more technical in nature. Insects are highly erratic in the air, so first it is necessary to persuade them to fly into the field of view of the camera. Then the shutter must be opened at the exact instant they loom into focus.

To put this into context, a fast-flying insect heading towards a camera lens will snap into focus and out again within 1/500 of a second. This compares with about one quarter of a second taken for the nerve signal to travel from the photographer's eye to the brain, and for the brain to instruct the shutter finger to press. A further eighth of a second must be added to this for a typical SLR camera mechanism to operate. Thus even if the hopeful photographer could visually register the fleeting moment when the insect flew into focus, it would have travelled about a metre past his shoulder before the shutter was open!

The solution to these problems lay in building a 'flight tunnel' wired with extremely sensitive light beams and detectors that operated a modified fast-opening shutter. The insect therefore took its own photograph by flying through one of the beams set at the point of focus.

This, however, was not the end of the matter. The final technical hurdle was to 'freeze' the insect's movement on film. Many insects fly with a wing-beat frequency in excess of two hundred cycles per second. This registers as a blur using the shutter speeds available on a camera. Nor are conventional flash guns of use to freeze the action, since they cannot deliver a suitably brief pulse with enough power. So it was necessary to build a series of flash guns (up to five are used simultaneously to reproduce the subtleties of natural light), each capable of producing a powerful light pulse lasting just 1/40,000 of a second. It was the briefness of this pulse, one fortieth that of a conventional flash, that froze all movement.

No amount of electronics is of any use, however, unless the subjects are willing. Insects only fly when conditions are just right, and working out each individual's needs involved trial and error. It may have meant laying on supplies of sugar-water for food or providing the right combination of temperature and light to lure them down the flight tunnel. Likewise I soon learnt that jumping spiders, which rely on a hydraulic action to leap, only performed if ample drinking water was on hand. In the end, the perplexing temperament of the electronic equipment and the idiosyncrasies of the animal subjects combined to provide days of despair, relieved occasionally by the joy of getting a good result. I have drawers full of transparencies in which the subject somehow eluded the equipment, perhaps showing only a wing or antenna protruding from the edge of the frame. Dozens, if not hundreds, of takes were required to achieve results of the right pictorial strength.

A particularly prolonged high-speed project was to capture the bellbird in flight. This was conducted outdoors, where a wild bird was persuaded, of its own will, to fly a precise route before landing on the target branch. The various flash guns, beams, detectors and wiring had then to be put in place one by one so as not to cause the bird to change its flight path. This went relatively according to plan, but when the moment came to start operating the flashes I discovered I had underestimated the bellbird's learning ability. It soon came to know exactly where the 'invisible' light beam and detector were because of the flash guns going off. It would then, by dint of some wonderful aerobatics, manage to fly around the beam, so failing to trip my equipment. Thus followed a game of cat and mouse, with me shifting the beams to ambush the bellbird, and it learning the new position.

Three weeks of patience finally won out with the bellbird. But there are times when events conspire to defeat all hopes, and there is nothing to do but philosophically pack up and go home. After days of work, the subject may shift roost or even migrate to the other side of the globe. Wild animals do not fit human agendas. They move in a universe separate from our own — and so it should be.